D1069165

A Child's Garden of Graffiti

A Child's Garden of Graffiti.

Compiled by Thomas W. Tickell

POP BOOKS

RANDOM HOUSE

Copyright © 1971, by Montcalm Prod., Inc.

All rights reserved under International
and Pan-American Copyright Laws

A Pop book. Published by Pop Books,
8721 Sunset Blvd., Suite C
Los Angeles, California 90069
and by Random House, Inc.
201 East 50th Street,
New York, N.Y. 10022

Library of Congress Catalogue Card Number: 72-171188

Printed in U.S.A

Photographs and design by Hy Fujita

DON'T FLY UNITED
IN PUBLIC.

YOUR FLY IS OPEN.
Yes...but not to anyone.

Joan of Arc.
was a Lesbian.

And a spitfire.
H.J.

Send a comb
to Allen Ginsberg

Robin Hood
made
Marian.

RAYMOND
DOMENICO

FOR THE NEW GENERATION!

Eddie Fisher is a winner.

— Connie

Yes, but the winner of my
discontent.

— Liz.

THE NEW GENERATION!
THE NEW GENERATION!
THE NEW GENERATION!

ILLEGAL
TO BACK OUT
ON TO FIGUEROA ST.

This car is constipated.
It hasn't passed anything all day.

Darwin's father was a Monkey.

GOD IS DEAD.
NIETZSCHE

Nietzsche is dead.
—God

THE HELL I AM.
—NIETZSCHE

You HAVEN'T HEARD THE OF LAST ME GOD

To make soup,
Take a look...
Then wash your hand

Et tu you brute?

The Count of Monte Cristo, was a Closet Queen.

BILLY SUNDAY IS JEWISH.

But then who isn't?

Me.
—Lester Maddox

Me Too.
—Omar Shariff

"I'll Say"
Barbra.

LITTLE JACK HORNER
WAS VERY JADED
INDEED.

THE LITTLE OLD
LADY WHO LIVED
IN THE SHOE
RECOMMENDS
THE PILL.

Jack Spratt was
a wife-snapper.

NO PARKING

UNAUTHORIZED VEHICLES
WILL BE TOWED AWAY
AT OWNER'S EXPENSE !!

Mother Hubbard is a sadist.

HUMPTY DUMPTY GOT
BUSTED FOR HAVING A SIT-IN
ON THE KING'S WALL.

Mother Goose
loves to be.

PERRY COMO IS A NERVOUS WRECK.

VENUS DE MILD NEVER PUT HER HAND TO ANYTHING.

Everything...like

Rejoines.

Incest.

THE NEW GENERATION THE NEW GENERATION THE NEW GENERATI

Dracula is
alive and
thirsty

JACK AND JILL ARE OVER THE HI...

DRAC IS A
PAIN IN THE
NECK!

Roses are red
Violets are blue
Nancy loves Ronnie
Do you ??
NO!
7UP
Out to Lunch
Margaret Mitchell,
hush yore mouf !!!

SPIRO RHYMES WITH ZERO.
R.M.

DRAFT
BEER,
NOT
BOYS!

Pablo Casals plays
his instrument with a beau.

Cancel Monday
Mornings.

Snow White is kinky
for midgets.

A free pet?
You're sure?

Caesar had a lot of Gaul

4853

A funny thing
happened on my
way through
the forehead.

—Athena

ROMULUS HAD
FALLEN ARCHES.

Media had the
solution to the generation
gap. SO DID OEDIPUS.

MY PARENTS ARE 69.
THANK GOD THEY DON'T
OPEN YOUR MAIL.

The Pied Piper was
a pederast.

VICTOR BORGE
MOONLIGHTS AS
A PIANO TUNER.

· DEFENSE D'AFFICHER ·

THIS IS BROTHERHOOD WEEK.... TAKE A DYKE TO DINNER.

❀

Colonel Sanders chokes on chicken. Lester Maddox should choke on chicken.

George Wallace passes for white.

White is off-color.

Yes, Santa Claus, there is a Virginia — and some of her is very bigoted.

Heloise Hates Abelard.
ALSO HINTS.

1939

ART KRAFT IS THE
SPAWN OF ARTSY-KRAFTSY

FOLD ME,
SPINDLE ME,
MUTILATE ME.
— Marquis de Sade.

Show me a home
where the buffalo roam,
and I'll show you
Phyllis Diller's
Apartment.

919

BEVERLY HILLS
IS A CULTURAL
WASTELAND.

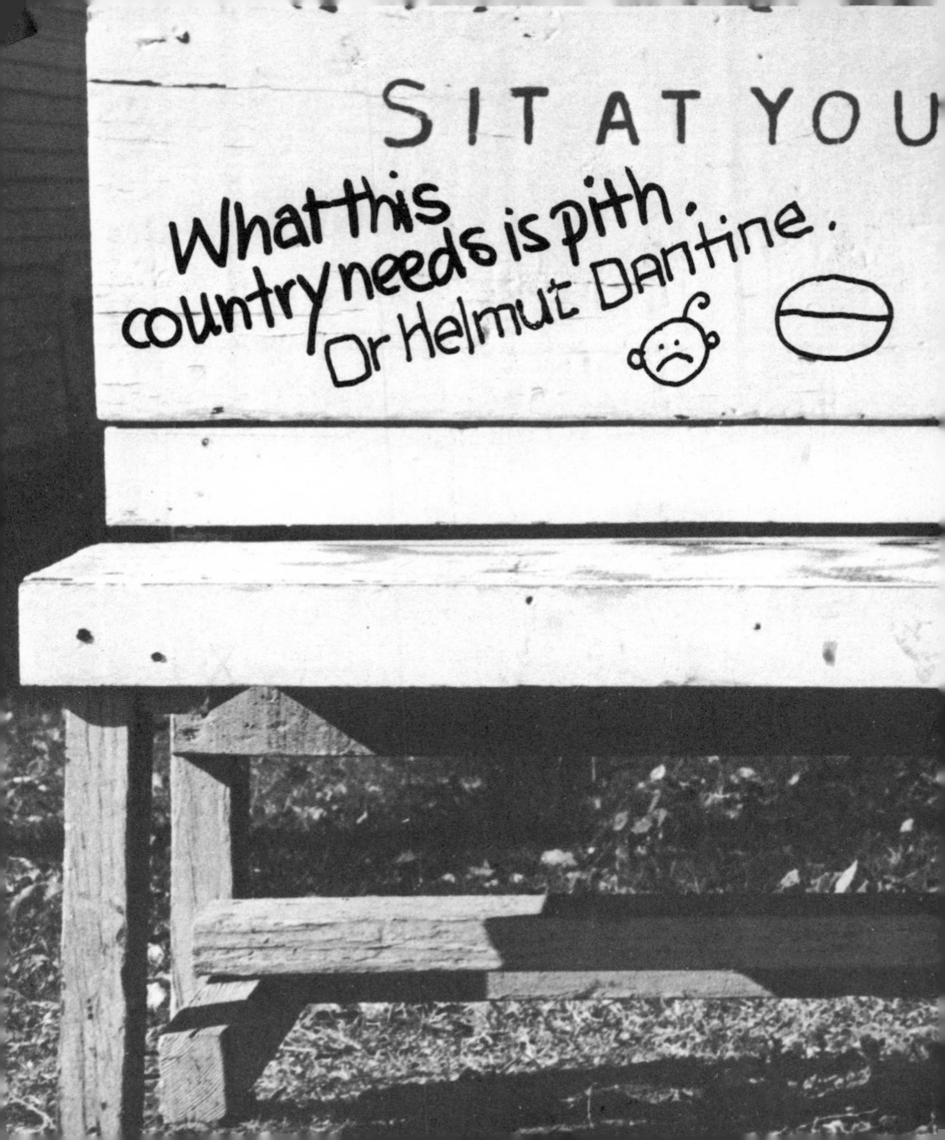
SIT AT YOU
What this country needs is pith.
Dr Helmut Dantine.

JESUS SAVES at Stinholtz Savings and Loan.

HARI KARI CAN BE FUN. HARI KRISHNA CAN BE BORING.

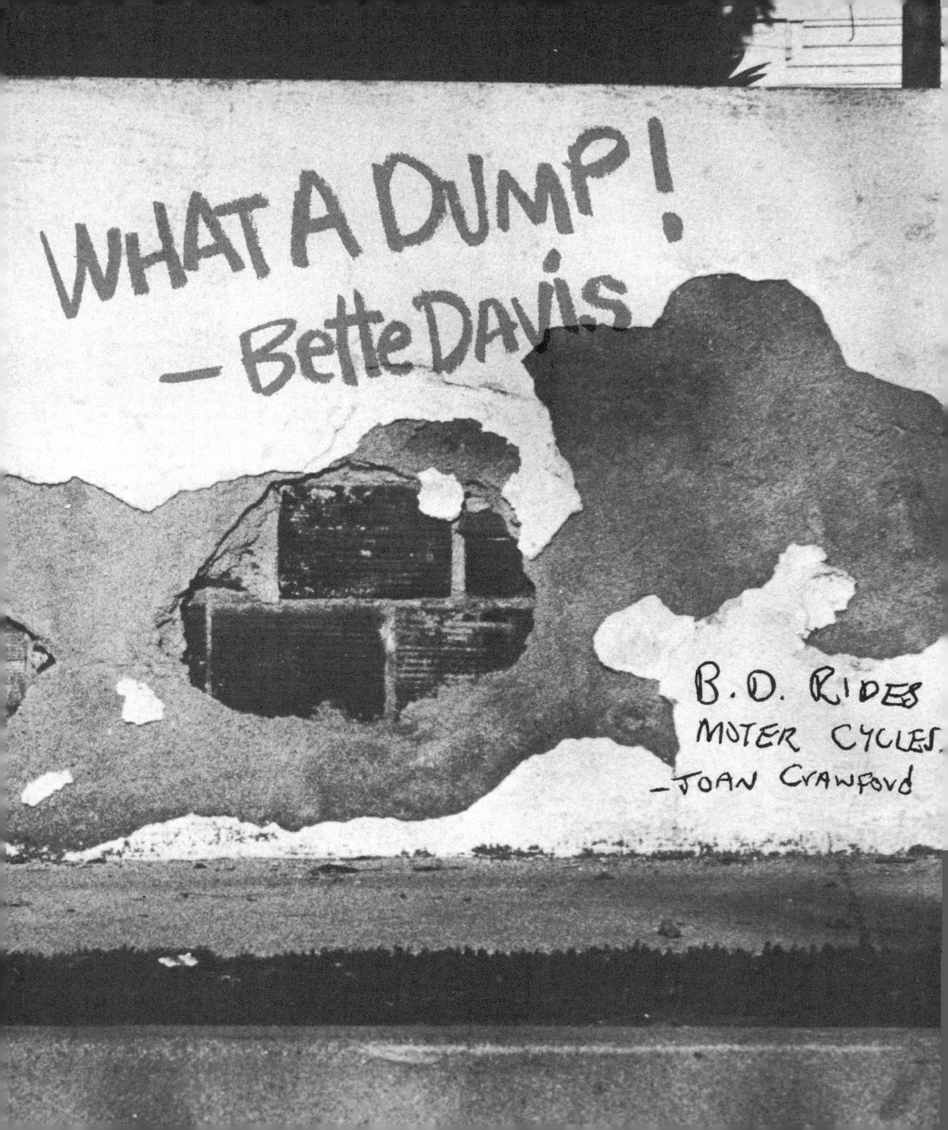
WHAT A DUMP!
— Bette Davis
B.O. RIDES
MOTER CYCLES.
-JOAN CRAWFORD

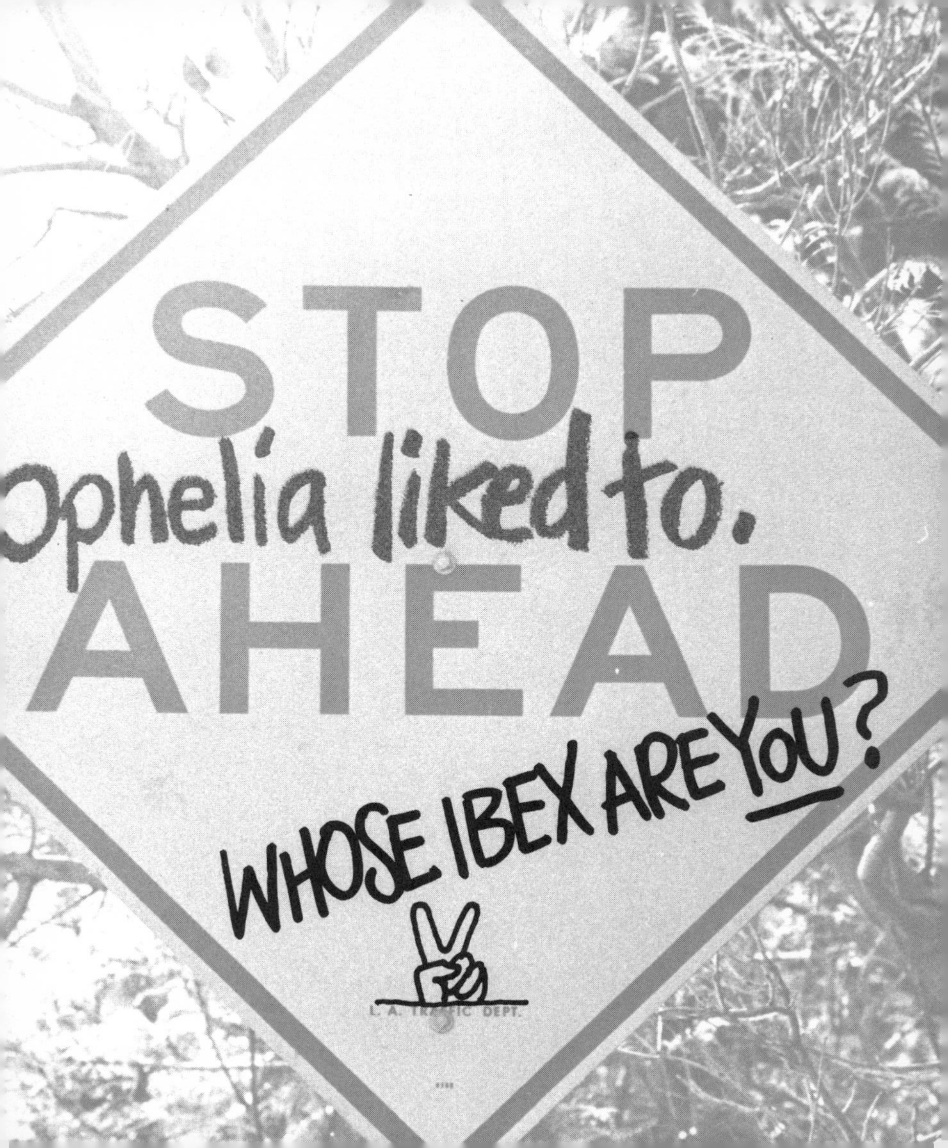
STOP
Ophelia liked to.
AHEAD
WHOSE IBEX ARE YOU?
L. A. TRAFFIC DEPT.

If you don't vote
for me I'll hold
my breath.
—Shirley Temple

YOU'LL ALWAYS BE THE
CREAM IN MY TAP-TAP-TAPIOCA
—ANN MILLER

A Woman's work is never done
— Connie Stevens —

REX REED LIVES IN THE 21ST CENTURY.

If at first you don't succeed, pull yourself up by your ankle straps.
— Joan Crawford

Ahead to DIVISION ST. The
Clean up America.
SPIRO AGNEW IS A
LIMP WRISTWATCH
T.S. ELIOT + D.H. LAWRENCE

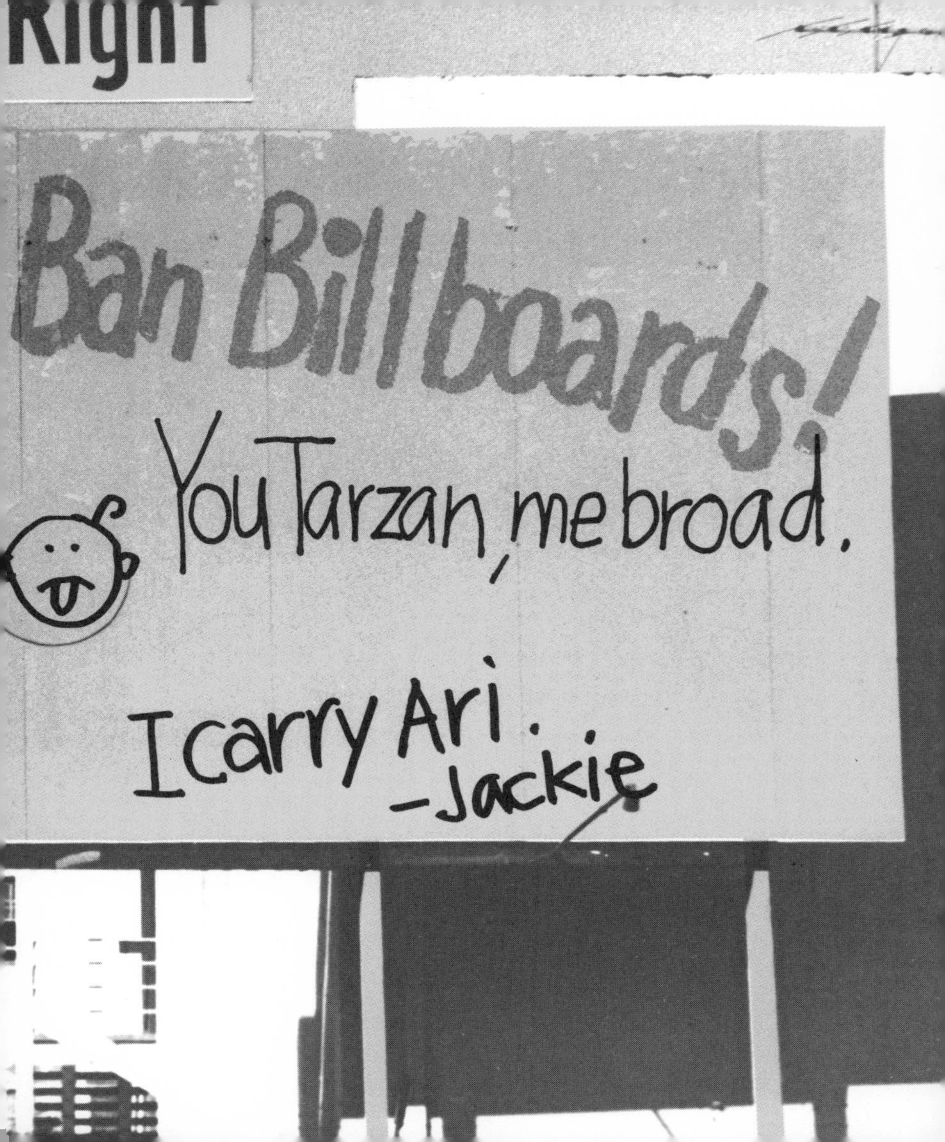
Right
Ban Billboards!
You Tarzan, me broad.
I carry Ari.
-Jackie

the ~~#~~ Sales Manager Is on the floor With a Customer.

or thwin.

THINK

UP WITH MINI SKIRTS.
OFF

CHICKEN LITTLE IS A JOKE.

CINDERELLA WAS

EXPORT ACNE

Daddy, what's a cu

DO YOUR GOOD DEED FOR TODAY

CLEAN A

mquat?

A GOLD DIGGER.

Hannibal's elephants
messed up the Alps.

NOAH WEBSTER COULDN'T
SPEAK ENGLISH.

Send the
Asian flu
back where
it came from.

CAMEL'S TEETH.

WILLIAM IS A LOUSY

A Yippie is a Snippy hippie.

BUCKLEY SPELLER.

Ethel Merman, Shut up already.

The
BURN-THE-BRA
MOVEMENT IS AN AWFUL
LETDOWN.

GREGORY PECK
IS A BUSHEL
OF LAUGHS.

Help stamp out
Reader's Digestism.

I am known
a heterosexual
Ronald Reagan

PAGING MRS. EWING SCOTT.

Angie Dickinson wears support hose.

PAUL NEWMAN HAS BROWN EYES!!! AND WEARS BLUE CONTACTS.

Support Sophia Loren

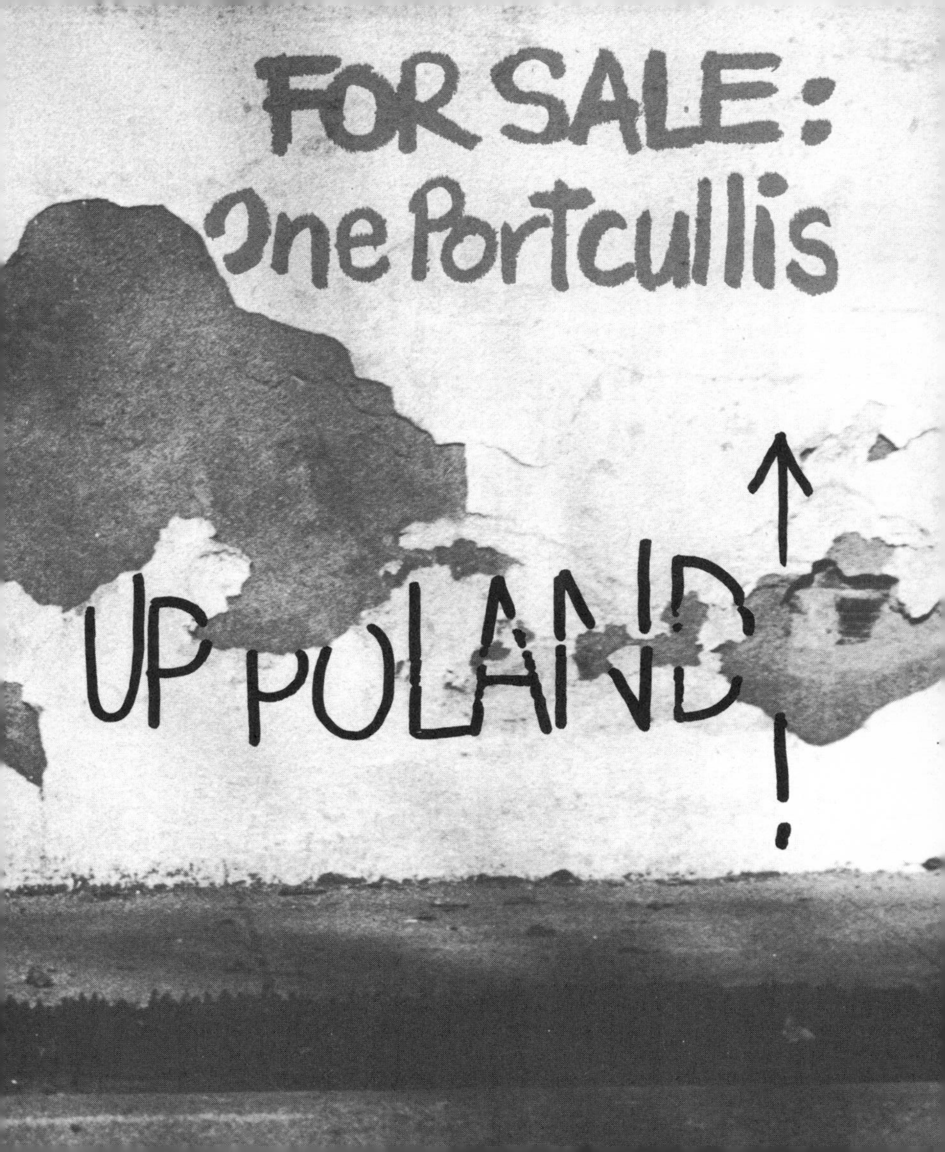
FOR SALE:
One Portcullis
UP POLAND!

WHERE CAN I FIND PANDORA'S BOX?

MY
MOTHER MADE ME A
HOMOSEXUAL.

Did he have feet of clay?

If I buy enough silly
Putty will she make
one for me?

DOGS
MUST BE KEPT
ON LEASH
MUN. CODE · SEC. 63.55

Dolly Madison put

I came I saw I turped.

REBECCA OF
SUNNYBROOK FARM
COULDN'T RAISE
RADISHES.

FOR
ENT

Oregano in her ice cream.

RAQUEL WELCH
HAS ADENOIDS.
Boy, does she have adenoids!

Godzilla has
halitosis.
He cured it when he discovered
Nair.

NO
VEHICLES
ALLOWED

Bed is better
than ever.

Plagiarism is a
four-letter word.
—Francis Bacon

BACON IS A FIVE LETTER WORD.
—Joe Egg

THE
MARQUIS
de SADE
WAS A
EUNUCH.

A KARATE CHOP
SHOULD NOT
NECESSARILY BE
BROILED.

A copse is for copulating.
I wish I hadn't said that.

Elizabeth Taylor was chaste.

chased.

T-T-thats all Folks !!!